Amazing Animals
Rhinoceroses

Please visit our Web site, www.garethstevens.com. For a free color catalog of all our high-quality books, call toll free 1-800-542-2595 or fax 1-877-542-2596.

Library of Congress Cataloging-in-Publication Data

Ciovacco, Justine.
  Rhinoceroses / Justine Ciovacco.
      p. cm. — (Amazing animals)
  Includes index.
  ISBN 978-1-4339-4023-1 (pbk.)
  ISBN 978-1-4339-4024-8 (6-pack)
  ISBN 978-1-4339-4022-4 (library binding)
  1. Rhinoceroses—Juvenile literature. I. Title.
  QL737.U63C56 2010
  599.66'8—dc22
                                    2010000492

This edition first published in 2011 by
Gareth Stevens Publishing
111 East 14th Street, Suite 349
New York, NY 10003

This edition copyright © 2011 Gareth Stevens Publishing.
Original edition copyright © 2006 by Readers' Digest Young Families.

Editor: Greg Roza
Designer: Christopher Logan

Photo credits: Cover, back cover, pp. 4–5, 8–9, 16–17, 18 (bottom left), 18–19, 30–31, 36 (bottom left), 46 Shutterstock.com; pp. 1, 3 Photodisc/ Getty Images; pp. 6–7 © iStockphoto.com/J. White; pp. 9 (bottom right), 17 (bottom), 38–39 © Digital Vision; pp. 10–11 © iStockphoto.com/Diane Diederich; pp. 12–13, 22 (bottom), 31 (bottom), 42–43 © Dynamic Graphics Inc.; pp. 14–15 © Image Source; pp. 20–21 © Nova Development Corporation; pp. 22–23 © iStockphoto.com/H. Tuller; pp. 24–25 © iStockphoto.com/Adam Pacey; pp. 26–27 © Corbis; p. 27 (bottom) © iStock-photo.com/Stephen Meese; p. 28 (bottom) © iStockphoto.com/Jeremy Voisey; pp. 28–29 © iStockphoto.com/Gerri Hernández; pp. 32–33 © Jupiter Images; pp. 34–35 © Corel Corporation; pp. 36–37 © IT Stock; pp. 44–45 © iStockphoto.com/Todd Aarnes.

Printed in the United States of America

CPSIA compliance information: Batch #CS10GS: For further information contact Gareth Stevens, New York, New York at 1-800-542-2595.

Amazing Animals
Rhinoceroses

By Justine Ciovacco

 **Gareth Stevens**
Publishing

Contents

Chapter 1
A Rhinoceros Grows Up

So Much Milk

Rhino calves drink an amount of milk equal to 20 full glasses each day.

It's just another hot, dry afternoon on the African plain for everyone except one female white rhinoceros. She had been lying near a shallow pool of water with other female rhinos. Now she walks away to part of the grassland that's quiet and safe. It has been 517 days—almost 1½ years—since she first became **pregnant**, and she is almost ready to give birth.

After a few days, she gives birth to one baby. Mama Rhinoceros cleans her new son with soft, firm licks. She stands over him and watches his every move. Baby Rhinoceros can stand within an hour after birth. Soon he tucks his head under his mother's belly and drinks her milk. He needs milk to grow and be strong. A few hours later, he's ready to go for a walk.

Big Baby

A newborn white rhinoceros weighs 110 pounds (50 kg) at birth. That's about as heavy as 15 human babies!

For the next few weeks, Baby Rhinoceros and his mother stay by themselves while he grows. Sometimes they walk through the dry grassland together. Mama walks a few steps ahead to protect her little one against sudden danger. Lions and tigers hunt baby rhinos, but they're rarely a match for a mother rhino.

Baby Rhino chomps on grass and other plants, just like his mother. Every few hours, he drinks milk. When Mama Rhinoceros thinks her son is ready to meet other rhinos, she nudges him into areas where there are rhinos she knows. But if anyone gets too close to her baby, Mama Rhinoceros quickly steps between them.

Baby Rhinoceros's horns begin to grow when he is 5 weeks old. He and his mother spend most of their day with a small group of rhinos. Mama watches closely as he plays with other babies nearby.

Wild Words

A female rhinoceros is called a cow. A male is called a bull. Their baby is called a calf.

Daddy Time

By age 10, a male rhinoceros is ready to become a father.

For the next 2 years, Baby Rhinoceros stays with his mother. He continues to rest near her and drink her milk. She still tries to protect him from **predators**.

Baby Rhinoceros knows it's time to leave his mother's side when she is pregnant again. He wanders farther from her each day until she is ready to give birth. He likes spending more time by himself. Soon he decides he wants his own piece of land.

Baby Rhinoceros finds land that doesn't smell like the **urine** or **dung** of other rhinos. When he finds the perfect spot, he sprays his urine all around. Then he makes large piles of dung and stomps on them with his feet. Finally, he walks around his **territory** so he can spread his dung on the land. Now all rhinos can smell that this is his area. He has made his own home sweet home!

One Smell Can Tell

Female rhinoceroses walk anywhere they want. So do males, but they can't stay too long in areas that smell like other male rhinos. A male rhinoceros marks his territory to let other rhinos know he owns the place.

Chapter 2

The Body of a Rhinoceros

On Tiptoe!

Rhinoceroses walk and run on tiptoe! Each foot has three toes, and each toe is protected by a thick hoof.

Rhinoceroses are the second-largest land **mammals** on Earth. Only elephants are larger.

Big Bodies

The first thing you notice about a rhinoceros is how big and blocky it is. Rhinos are tall—up to 6 feet (1.8 m) high—and wide! They can weigh up to 4 tons (3.6 t)!

Rhinoceroses have heavy, thick skin. Their skin protects them from sharp twigs and thorns that could scratch them as they walk through tall grass and between bushes and trees. A rhinoceros has hair on its ears and the end of its tail. It also has eyelashes.

Surprisingly Swift

Despite their large size, rhinoceroses can run as fast as 30 miles (48 km) an hour for short distances. That's about the speed of a car on a city street. Like their horse relatives, rhinos gallop on their toes. This helps them run faster.

Five of a Kind

There are five rhinoceros **species**. The biggest is the white rhinoceros. It's not really white, just like the black rhinoceros isn't black. Both are shades of gray and live in Africa.

The other three species live in Southeast Asia. Javan and Indian rhinoceroses look like they're wearing armor. They have thick folds of skin over their shoulders and rear end. The skin is more **flexible** in the folded areas, helping the rhinos move more easily. The Indian rhinoceros also has bumps on its skin.

The smallest rhino is the Sumatran rhinoceros. It's sometimes called the "hairy rhinoceros." Young Sumatran rhinos have patches of shaggy, reddish brown hair on their backs and sides. As they grow older, their hair turns darker and often falls off.

Color Change

This white rhinoceros shows how rhino skin color can change as the animal grows older. Part of the color change depends on how much time the rhinoceros has spent **wallowing** in mud or dirt.

The skin of Indian rhinoceroses looks like a suit of armor. They are the only rhinoceroses with bumps on their skin.

Rhino horns are so thick, sharp, and strong that some can cut through metal!

Heavy Horns

The word *rhinoceros* comes from two Greek words and means "nose horn." All rhinoceroses have at least one horn on top of their nose. White, black, and Sumatran rhinoceroses have two horns. The horn at the front of the nose is usually larger than the one behind it. A rhinoceros's horn is made of **keratin**, which is the same tough material your nails are made of.

Rhinoceroses use their horns to jab other rhinos that get too close. Rhinos are rougher with their horns when they fight. The horns are also helpful in pulling down tall bushes and tree branches. Sometimes rhinos dig up dirt with their horns. They might be looking for salt, water, or food.

Rhinoceros horns start to grow when calves are about 5 weeks old. They grow out of the rhino's skin and never stop growing! Each year, a rhinoceros's horn grows about 3 to 8 inches (8 to 20 cm). If a rhino's horn breaks off, it grows back.

Humongous Horn
The horn of a white rhino can be 5 feet (1.5 m) long!

Rhinoceros Senses

Rhinos can't see very well. A rhinoceros's tiny eyes are on either side of its head. This makes it hard to see things straight ahead. The rhino must turn its head from side to side and look out of one eye at a time. Rhinos sometimes run into trees and rocks!

However, a rhinoceros has an excellent sense of smell. It's big nostrils can pick up scents as far as eight football fields away! Mothers and calves know each other's scent. The scent of a predator causes rhinos to move away quickly.

The ears of a rhinoceros are on top of its head. This helps it hear sounds from far away. A rhino can turn its ears to hear sounds from different directions.

Tales of the Tail

A rhino's tail is short, with stiff hairs that hang down at the end. If a rhino is scared, it sometimes curls its tail into a corkscrew shape.

A rhinoceros's thick, straight legs help support the animal's massive size and weight. But they make lying down difficult. A rhino bends its back legs into a slight kneel and then lowers the rest of its body until it is lying down in a heap.

Myth Maker

Some people think the myth of the unicorn might have been based on a type of rhinoceros that lived thousands of years ago in southern Russia and the Ukraine. It was a long, tall animal with a 7-foot (2-m) horn on its forehead.

Chapter 3
Rhinoceros Life

Rubbing Rhinos

Rhinoceroses like to rub their big bodies against trees and bushes when they have an itch. Rubbing also leaves a rhino's scent behind.

Wallowing in mud and dirt helps rhinoceroses protect their skin from the sun and insect bites. It's also a great way to cool off on a hot day.

All in a Day

Most rhinoceroses live alone, but they usually gather in areas where there is food, water, and mud. White rhinos are the only species that forms small groups. These groups have no more than six animals. They spend a few hours together each day eating and drinking.

Rhinoceroses graze most of the day and take breaks. Black and white rhinos in Africa may not eat much until after the sun goes down. They can sleep standing up, but they often try to lie down in the shade.

Indian rhinoceroses are good swimmers. They live in swampy jungle areas and bathe every day. These rhinos push their way through the jungle plants to get to water. Other animals follow their paths.

Big Swimmers

Indian rhinos are great swimmers. They can even dive and eat underwater. Javan rhinos have even been seen swimming in the Indian Ocean!

Picking a Fight

Rhinoceroses are so big that people assume they must be tough. But rhinos don't like to fight. If left alone, rhinoceroses usually won't attack. Of all the species, black rhinoceroses are most likely to fight. If they smell anything unusual, they charge forward. This reaction has scared many humans who were trying to get a closer look!

Rhinoceroses sometimes fight with each other. Males battle for a female or to take over a piece of land. Male and female rhinos sometimes fight when they first meet each other. The female may not like the male's way of giving her attention. She may attack to make him stay away. It rarely works for long.

Ready, Set, Charge!

When young rhinos play-fight, they learn the basics of attacking. As an adult, an attacking rhino first lowers its head and may snort. Then it races forward at speeds up to 30 miles (48 km) an hour. A galloping rhino can cause serious damage, even death.

Female rhinoceroses use their horns to charge at predators that come near their children.

When it wants to show that it's in charge, a rhinoceros may go horn to horn with another rhinoceros and make a low growl.

Sound Off

Rhinoceroses use many sounds to communicate. Males and females whistle and snort to get each other's attention. Rhinos in a fight may grunt or scream. Rhinoceroses that are upset sometimes squeal or growl.

Black rhinoceroses make the most sounds of all rhinos. The babies squeak. Adults make loud bursts of sound that other rhinos far away can hear. But you wouldn't hear them! The loudest sound a black rhino makes is below the range of human hearing.

White rhinoceroses make huffing sounds that scientists can hear only with special machines. But other rhinos can hear them, even over great distances. Scientists say the sounds are similar to the low noises elephants make.

Bird Buddies

Rhinoceroses in Africa have special feathered friends. Oxpeckers, which are also called tick birds, sit on a rhino's back and eat ticks off the rhino's skin. A rhino knows danger may be near if a bird calls out suddenly or flies away.

Chapter 4
What Rhinoceroses Eat

The white rhinoceros is sometimes called the square-lipped rhinoceros because of the shape of its mouth.

Made for Megameals

Rhinoceroses eat up to 110 pounds (50 kg) of plants a day. Their flexible necks and long heads help rhinos reach leaves on trees and tall bushes. White rhinoceroses have a small bump of strong muscles behind their head. The bump helps them raise and lower their big heads as they eat.

All rhinoceroses have teeth for crushing and chewing plants on the sides of their mouth. An adult rhino has between 24 and 34 teeth. Black and white rhinos have no front teeth.

White rhinoceroses have a wide, square-shaped upper lip that lets them clip off whole patches of short grasses. Their name comes from their mouth. Dutch settlers called them *wijd*, which means "wide." English speakers misunderstood the word and thought it was *white*.

Big Eater

The rhinoceros is one of the world's largest grazing animals.

Fighting Fangs

Indian, Javan, and Sumatran rhinos have long, tusklike front teeth. They use them for eating and fighting.

Food for Rhinos

Black and white rhinoceroses live in Africa, mainly on grasslands and in areas with bushes and trees. Black rhinoceroses eat branches and leaves. White rhinoceroses eat grasses.

Javan rhinoceroses live in the rain forests of Asia. They eat leaves, young plants, and twigs. They bend down young trees and branches with fruit until they break off, forming a nice meal. Sumatran rhinoceroses live in the rain forest and on wooded mountain slopes. Their favorite foods are bamboo, figs, and mangoes.

Indian rhinoceroses live in swampy areas surrounded by thick patches of grass. Their lips fold to one side so they can easily tear grass and plants out of the ground.

Water Works

Rhinoceroses need to drink water often to replace what they lose when they sweat and urinate.

The upper lip of a black rhinoceros is pointed, which lets the rhino grab tall plants and pull them into its mouth.

Chapter 5
Rhinoceroses in the World

Where Rhinoceroses Live

ASIA

Nepal

India

Vietnam

Malaysia

Sumatra

Java

AFRICA

Sudan

Dem. Rep.
of Congo

Rwanda

Zambia

Namibia

Botswana

South Africa

Uganda

Kenya

Tanzania

Malawi

Mozambique

Zimbabwe

Swaziland

The **dark green** areas show where black rhinoceroses live.

The **blue** areas show where white rhinoceroses live.

The **pink** areas show where both white and black rhinoceroses live.

The **purple** area shows where Indian rhinoceroses live.

The **red** areas show where Javan rhinoceroses live.

The **light green** areas show where Sumatran rhinoceroses live.

Past and Present

Rhinoceroses have been on Earth for 40 million years. There were once more than 30 kinds of rhinos living in North America, Europe, Africa, and Asia. People hunted them for sport and for their horns. Today, there are only five kinds of rhinos in the world. White and black rhinos live in Africa. They both live on flat lands among many grasses and plants. The Sumatran, Indian, and Javan rhinos live in Asia. The Sumatran rhino lives in tropical rain forests and along wooded mountain slopes in Sumatra, Borneo, and Malaysia. Indian rhinos live in Nepal and northeast India. Javan rhinos live on the jungle island of Java and in other parts of Southeast Asia.

Most rhinos live in national parks and **reserves**. These land areas are set up by governments and groups of people to protect the rhinos in their natural **habitats**.

Rhino Populations

white rhinos: 11,330
black rhinos: 3,610
Indian rhinos: 2,500
Sumatran rhinos: 300
Javan rhinos: 60

Rhinoceroses in Danger

Most rhinoceros species are in danger of becoming **extinct**. People have been killing these giant creatures for millions of years. Recently, people have taken over their land to build farms and cut down trees in rain forests. This makes it hard for rhinos to find food or homes.

People also hunt rhinos for their horns, which can be sold for high prices. Some people believe the horns can help fight illnesses. They grind the horns into a powder and add them to medicines. Others use the horns to make knife handles.

Fast Facts About White Rhinoceroses

Scientific name	*Ceratotherium simum*
Class	Mammalia
Order	Perissodactyla
Size	Up to 14 feet (4.3 m) long
Weight	Up to 8,000 pounds (3,600 kg)
Life span	30 to 40 years
Habitat	Grasslands and woodlands
Speed	30 miles (48 km) per hour in bursts

It's now illegal to hunt rhinos and sell their horns, but some people still do it. They're called **poachers**.

Glossary

dung—solid waste from an animal's body

extinct—no longer existing

flexible—easily moveable

fossilize—to change into a fossil

habitat—the natural environment where an animal or plant lives

keratin—the matter from which animals' hair, nails, and horns are made

mammal—an animal with a backbone and hair on its body that drinks milk from its mother when it is a baby

The Largest of the Land

An ancient species of rhinoceros was the largest land mammal ever to live on Earth! It was nearly 18 feet (5.5 m) high, 36 feet (11 m) long, and weighed about 10 tons (9 t)! Scientists know this from **fossilized** bones of the *Indricotherium* that were found in central Asia.

poacher—a person who illegally kills or captures wild animals

predator—an animal that hunts and eats other animals to survive

pregnant—carrying an unborn baby in the body

reserve—an area of land set aside for animals to live in safety

species—a group of plants or animals that are the same

territory—an area of land that an animal considers to be its own and will fight to defend

urine—a yellow liquid containing water and waste products that flows out of an animal's body

wallow—to roll around in a relaxed way

Rhinoceroses: Show What You Know

How much have you learned about rhinoceroses? Grab a piece of paper and a pencil and write your answers down.

1. How long does it take a mother rhino to give birth after mating?

2. How much does a newborn white rhino weigh?

3. What is the largest rhinoceros species?

4. Which types of rhinoceroses live in Southeast Asia?

5. At what age is a male rhino ready to become a father?

6. Which species of rhinoceros is most likely to fight?

7. What do rhinoceroses eat, and how much do they eat in 1 day?

8. How many teeth does an adult rhino have?

9. How long have rhinoceroses been on Earth?

10. How much can white rhinoceroses weigh?

1. About 517 days 2. About 110 pounds (50 kg) 3. The white rhinoceros 4. Javan, Indian, and Sumatran rhinoceroses 5. About age 10 6. The black rhinoceros 7. About 110 pounds (50 kg) of plants 8. Between 24 and 34 teeth 9. 40 million years 10. Up to 8,000 pounds (3,600 kg)

For More Information

Books

Czech, Jan M. *The Rhino*. Berkeley Heights, NJ: Enslow Publishers, 2005.

Firestone, Mary. *Top 50 Reasons to Care About Rhinos: Animals in Peril*. Berkeley Heights, NJ: Enslow Publishers, 2010.

Walker, Sally M. *Rhinos*. Minneapolis, MN: Lerner Publications, 2007.

Web Sites

Black Rhino—An Endangered Species
www.bagheera.com/inthewild/van_anim_rhino.htm
Learn what is being done to protect rhinos in the wild.

Rhinoceros
www.kidskonnect.com/subject-index/13-animals/409-rhinoceros.html
Find links to many sites about rhinos.

Publisher's note to educators and parents: Our editors have carefully reviewed these Web sites to ensure that they are suitable for students. Many Web sites change frequently, however, and we cannot guarantee that a site's future contents will continue to meet our high standards of quality and educational value. Be advised that students should be closely supervised whenever they access the Internet.

Index